AF866977

Paper FTX

Foundations in Taxation

(Finance Act 2025)

Pocket notes

KAPLAN
PUBLISHING

British library cataloguing-in-publication data

A catalogue record for this book is available from the British Library.

Published by:
Kaplan Publishing UK
Unit 2 The Business Centre
Molly Millars Lane
Wokingham
Berkshire
RG41 2QZ

ISBN 978-1-83735-022-3

Printed and bound in Great Britain.

Contents

Preface

These pocket notes contain the key points you need to know for the examination, presented in a unique visual way that makes revision easy and effective.

Written by experienced lecturers and authors, these pocket notes break down content into manageable chunks to maximise your concentration.

Quality and accuracy are of the utmost importance to us so if you spot an error in any of our products, please send an email to mykaplanreporting@kaplan.com with full details, or follow the link to the feedback form in MyKaplan.

Our Quality Co-ordinator will work with our technical team to verify the error and take action to ensure it is corrected in future.

A guide to the exam

FTX is a two hour computer based examination.

The pass mark is 50%.

The paper is in two parts and all the questions are compulsory.

The paper is predominantly computational.

- Section A will contain 15 compulsory multiple choice questions worth 2 marks each, for a total of 30 marks.
- Section B will contain 8 questions for a total of 70 marks.
- Section B will contain 2 questions worth 15 marks, 2 questions worth 10 marks and 4 questions worth 5 marks.
- One of the 15 mark questions in section B will focus on income tax and the other 15 mark question will focus on corporation tax. The remaining questions will examine topics from any area of the syllabus.

Additional information

Examinations in June 2026, December 2026 and June 2027 will examine legislation up to and including Finance Act 2025 (which received Royal Assent on 20 March 2025).

Calculations should be made to the nearest month and the nearest £.

The keys to success

- Learn and follow the pro formas for computational questions.
- Always show workings in relevant questions.
- Adopt a logical approach and cross reference workings to the main computation to keep your answer clear.
- Spend the time learning the specific rules on areas such as disallowable expenditure, capital allowances, capital gains reliefs and benefits.
- As some questions can be on any topic, it is vital to study the entire syllabus and not just the basic principles.
- Watch out for articles from the examining team released in the Student Accountant magazine in the months up to your examination date. These give clues as to the areas that may be covered.
- Question practice!

Multiple choice questions

- Work steadily. Rushing leads to careless mistakes and questions are designed to include answers which result from common mistakes.
- If you don't know the answer, eliminate those options you know are incorrect and see if the answer becomes more obvious.
- Remember that only one answer to an multiple choice question can be right and there is no negative marking for an incorrect answer.
- After you have eliminated any options that you know to be wrong, if you are still unsure, guess.

chapter

1

Calculation of trading income

In this chapter

- Calculation of trading profits.
- Pro forma for cash basis.
- Pro forma for adjustment of profit (accruals basis).
- Disallowable expenditure – both bases.
- Disallowable expenditure – accruals basis.
- Allowable expenditure – both bases.
- Miscellaneous expenditure.
- Deductions under the accruals basis.
- Flat rate expenses.
- Tax year basis.

Calculation of trading profits

There are two methods of calculating the taxable trading profits for the accounting period:

- Cash basis (this is the default method)
- Accruals basis (trader can make an election to use the accruals basis).

Pro forma for cash basis

	£
Total cash receipts	X
Less Allowable expenses PAID	(X)
Less Capital Allowance on cars (if mileage allowances are not claimed)	(X)
Trading profit / (loss)	X/(X)

- There is no distinction between capital and revenue expenditure, therefore capital assets are treated as follows:
  - Purchases are allowable deductions when paid for (except cars, land and buildings).
  - Proceeds are treated as part of total taxable receipts when assets are sold.
  - Capital allowances are available for cars only; or flat rate expenses can be claimed instead.
- Certain expenses are not deductible.

Exam focus

Assume cash basis applies unless told otherwise.

Pro forma for adjustment of profit (accruals basis)

	£
Accounting net profit	X
Add back:	
Depreciation	X
Entertaining and gifts	X
Capital expenditure	X
Fines	X
Charitable donations	X
Goods removed from the business (selling price)	X
Allowable expenses	0
	X
Deduct:	
Allowable expenses not included in the accounts	(X)
Profits on the sale of non-current assets	(X)
Investment income	(X)
Capital allowances	(X)
Tax adjusted trading profit	X

Disallowable expenditure – both bases

These are items which are not allowable deductions when calculating taxable trading profits.

General principle	Disallow anything not incurred wholly and exclusively for the purposes of the trade
Fines	Disallow penalties re taxation or for infringing health and safety regulations
Donations	Disallow donations to political parties, national charities and gift aid donations
Legal expenses	Disallow if they relate to capital items re land and buildings However: • Allow the legal costs of renewing a short lease (50 years or less) • Allow the costs of registering patents and trademarks
Entertaining	Disallow the cost of entertaining customers and suppliers

Disallowable expenditure – accruals basis

These are also items which are not allowable deductions when calculating taxable trading profits under the accruals basis.

Under the accruals basis, as these, and the items on the previous page, would have been treated as expenses in the statement of profit or loss, they must now be added back – as shown in the accruals basis pro forma.

Capital expenditure	Add back improvements and initial 'repairs' expenditure to bring an asset into a fit state for use in the business
Depreciation	Add back accounting depreciation, together with any losses on the sale of non-current assets
Hire charges (high emission cars)	For cars with CO_2 emissions > 50g/km Disallow 15% × hire charge
Impairment losses	Add back losses not in relation to trade debts

Allowable expenditure – both bases

These are allowable deductions from trading profits and so under the cash basis are deducted fror trading receipts.

Under the accruals basis, these items will have already been treated as expenses in the statemen of profit or loss.

As the tax treatment for these items is the same as the accounting treatment, the item should be included in the accruals basis computation as a 0.

Do not add these items back in the pro forma for adjustment of profit under the accruals ba

General principle	Allow anything incurred wholly and exclusively for the purposes of the trade
Fines	Allow a deduction for parking fines incurred by employees while on company business
Donations	Allow small donations to local charities
Repairs	Allow repairs and redecoration
Legal expenses	Allow if they relate to trading items (e.g. collection of trade debts)
Gifts	Allow if they fulfil the following three conditions: • They incorporate a conspicuous advertisement for the business • The total cost per donee is not more than £50 per annum • The gift is not food, drink, tobacco or vouchers
Entertaining	Allow the cost of entertaining staff

Miscellaneous expenditure

Type of expenditure	Treatment	Notes
Compensation to employee for loss of office	Allow	Only if for benefit of trade
Cost of seconding employees to charities	Allow	
Counselling services provided in the UK for redundant employees	Allow	
Damages paid	Allow	Only if paid in connection with trade matter
Educational courses	Allow	Only if for trade purposes
Contributions to a registered pension scheme	Allow	Provided paid (not merely accrued) by the year end (even if using accruals basis)
Removal expenses	Allow	Provided not an expansionary move or expenses relating to personal move of proprietor
Salaries accrued at year end (under accruals basis)	Allow	Provided paid not more than nine months after year end
Travelling expenses to trader's place of business	Disallow	Unless trader has no fixed place of business
Patent royalties	Allow	
Pre trading expenditure	Allow	Must be revenue expense that would be allowable if trade had started and paid/incurred in the seven years before trade commenced

Deductions under the accruals basis

Income not taxable as trading income

- Rental income
- Dividend income
- Capital profits
- Interest received

Expenditure not included in the accounts but deductible for tax purposes

- Capital allowances
- The annual deduction for premium paid for grant of short lease on business premises:

Premium	X
Less: 2% × (n–1) × premium	(X)
Taxable on landlord	Y

$$\text{Deduction} = \frac{\text{Taxable on landlord (Y)}}{\text{Duration of lease in years}}$$

Flat rate expenses

These can be used:

- By sole trader or partnership
- Instead of deducting actual expenditure
- Under cash basis or accruals basis
- In two scenarios in the exam

Car expenses

- A trader incurs expenditure on a car for business use
- Can deduct approved mileage allowance
- Calculated on business mileage

First 10,000 miles	45p per mile
> 10,000 miles	25p per mile

Either deduct

- mileage allowance, OR
- business % of capital allowances and running costs,

but not both.

Personal use of business premises

- A trader runs a business such as guesthouse/B&B
- The trader lives in part of the business premises
- Can deduct total premises costs (services, rent, food, utilities)
- But reduce the deduction by a flat rate amount, reflecting private use
- The flat amount will be provided in the exam if needed
- Adjust private element of other expenses (eg mortgage interest) as normal.

Exam focus

The exam question will make clear whether flat rate expenses should be used.

Tax year basis

- Trading profits calculated for a period must be allocated to a tax year(s)
- Tax year basis taxes profits arising from 6 April to 5 April
- Profits of year end 31 March or 5 April 2026 – taxed in tax year 2025/26
- For other year ends, time apportion profits of two periods
- This may involve estimates for the second period

e.g

Example

Miriam prepares accounts to 31 December each year. Her trading results are:

Year ended 31 December 2025	£10,000
Year ended 31 December 2026 (forecast)	£15,000

For tax year 2025/26, she will be taxed on: (£10,000 × 9/12) + (£15,000 × 3/12) = £11,250

- If a trader starts trading during the tax year, tax profits arising from the start date to 5 April
- If a trader ceases trading during the tax year, tax profits from 6 April to date of cessation

chapter

2

Capital allowances

In this chapter

- Capital allowances pro forma.
- What qualifies as plant?
- What goes into the main pool?
- What goes into the special rate pool?
- Hire purchase assets.
- Writing down allowances.
- Annual investment allowance.
- First year allowance.
- Cars.
- Disposals.
- Cessation of trade.
- VAT.
- Short life assets.
- Structures and buildings allowances.

Capital allowances pro forma

		Main pool	Special rate pool	Short life asset	Private use asset	Allowances
	£	£	£	£	£	£
TWDV b/f		X	X	X		
Additions:						
Not qualifying for AIA or FYA:						
Cars (1 – 50g/km or second-hand zero-emission)		X				
Cars (over 50g/km)			X			
Car with private use					X	
Qualifying for AIA:						
Special rate pool	X					
AIA (Max £1,000,000 in total)	(X)					X
Transfer balance to special rate pool			X			
Plant and machinery	X					
AIA (Max £1,000,000 in total)	(X)					X
Transfer balance to main pool		X				
Less: Disposals (lower of original cost and sale proceeds)				(X)		
		X	X	X	X	

	£	Main pool £	Special rate pool £	Short life asset £	Private use asset £	Allowances £
BA / (BC)				X/(X)		X/(X)
Small pools WDA						
WDA at 18%		(X)				X
WDA at 6%			(X)			X
WDA at 6%/18% (depending on emissions)					(X) × BU%	X
Qualifying for FYA:						
New zero-emission cars	X					
FYA at 100%	(X)					X
		0				
TWDV c/f		X	X		X	
Total allowances						X

What qualifies as plant?

The term 'plant' is not defined in the legislation. However, the following items specifically qualify as plant under either case law or statute:

- swimming pool installed by owners of a caravan park
- movable partitioning in an office
- expenditure on acquiring computer software
- alteration of building for installation of plant.

Exam focus

Some items of plant qualify as integral features in buildings. You will be told in the examination if an asset falls into this category.

What goes into the main pool?

The main (general) pool contains everything **except**:

- Special rate pool items (see below)
- Any assets where there is private use by the proprietor (not by employees)
- Short life assets where a depooling election is made.

What goes into the special rate pool?

- Integral features in buildings.
- Cars with CO_2 emissions > 50g/km.
- Thermal insulation of a building.

Hire purchase assets

- Full cash price of asset brought into pool in period of first use.

Writing down allowances

Main pool

- 18% p.a. of the reducing balance.

Special rate pool

- 6% p.a. of the reducing balance.

Small Pools WDA

- WDA of up to £1,000 can be claimed on the main pool and/or special rate pool if the balance (after dealing with acquisitions and disposals in the period) is £1,000 or less.

Restrictions

- Time apportion only if the accounting period is less than (or more than) 12 months long.
- Never time apportion by reference to length of ownership.
- No WDA in the final period of trade.

Annual investment allowance

- AIA gives 100% relief on the first £1,000,000 of expenditure on P&M.
- Not available on any cars (regardless of CO_2 emissions).
- Time apportioned for long and short periods.
- Not available in AP when trade ceases.
- Should be allocated as follows:

  (1) Special rate pool additions

  (2) Main pool additions

  (3) Short life assets.

First Year Allowance (FYAs)

- 100% allowance in accounting period of purchase for expenditure on cars with zero CO_2 emissions.
- Never time apportioned if accounting period is not 12 months – always given in full.

e.g

Example

AIA/WDAs

In the year to 31 March 2026 the following transactions took place in a business using accruals basis:

14 October 2025	Plant which qualifies as an integral feature in a building is purchased for £970,000
30 December 2025	Plant sold for £800 (originally purchased for £4,000)
10 February 2026	Plant purchased for £72,000
17 March 2026	New zero-emission car purchased for £35,800

Compute the capital allowances for the year ended 31 March 2026 assuming that the pool balances on 1 April 2025 were:

Main pool	£4,900
Special rate pool	£12,000

	£	Main pool £	Special rate pool £	Allowances £
TWDV b/f		4,900	12,000	
Additions				
Qualifying for AIA				
Plant – Integral feature	970,000			
AIA	(970,000)			970,000
Transfer balance to special rate pool			0	
Qualifying for AIA				
Plant	72,000			
AIA (balance of £1,000,000)	(30,000)			30,000
Transfer balance to main pool		42,000		
Disposal		(800)		
		46,100	12,000	
WDA (18% × £46,100)		(8,298)		8,298
(6% × £12,000)			(720)	720
Qualifying for FYA				
Zero-emission car	35,800			
FYA at 100%	(35,800)			35,800
		0		
TWDV c/f		37,802	11,280	
Total allowances				1,044,818

Cars

Zero-emissions car	CO_2 emissions 1 – 50g/km	CO_2 emissions > 50g/km
• FYA if new • Put in main pool if second-hand • No AIA • Never time apportioned • Cannot have both FYA and WDA	• Put in the main pool • No AIA • WDA at 18%	• Put into special rate poo • No AIA • WDA at 6%

Private use cars – regardless of date of purchase

- Only relevant if private use is **by owner**, not employees
- Separate P.U. asset column
- WDA calculated according to CO_2 emissions and deducted in full in the P.U. asset column
- Only the business % can be claimed in the end allowances column

Under cash basis, capital allowances – cars only.

Other plant – deduct as an expense.

Example

Private use car

	£	
TWDV b/f	6,565	
WDA (18%)	(1,182)	× 70% business use = £827 allowance given in allowances column
TWDV c/f	5,383	

Disposals

Deduct lower of:

(i) sale proceeds, and

(ii) original cost

Main and special rate pool	Separate column
• If remaining balance is positive = continue to write down as normal	• If remaining balance is positive = balancing allowance
• If remaining balance is negative = balancing charge, add to profits	• If remaining balance is negative = balancing charge, add to profits
• No balancing allowance until the final year of trading	• Balancing adjustment is restricted to business % where some private use

Cessation of trade

On cessation capital allowances in the final period are calculated as follows:

- Acquisitions are added to the pool – no AIA, FYA or WDA.
- The lower of cost or disposal proceeds (or the market value of assets retained by the owner) are deducted.
- Balancing allowances or charges are given on each pool/asset.

VAT

If the business is registered for VAT it can reclaim VAT charged on capital assets except cars (unless they are 100% business use).

When capital assets are sold VAT will be charged, unless it was a car on which VAT can't be reclaimed.

When the costs provided in the question include VAT:

- If the business can reclaim the VAT – the cost of the asset for CAs must be NET of VAT.
- If the business can't reclaim the VAT – the cost of the asset for CAs must be INCLUSIVE of VAT.
- When assets are sold – the proceeds should be NET of VAT.
- VAT is charged at 20% (Chapter 11).

Short life assets

Type of asset?	Any item of plant, apart from cars, that is expected to decrease in value over a fairly short period.
Short life?	Expected to be disposed of within eight years of end of period of account in which the asset is acquired.
Election by?	Two years of end of period of account in which acquired (or 12m from 31 January following the tax year in which period of purchase ends, if income tax applies).
Why elect?	Asset will be put in a separate column rather than being included in the main pool. This enables the business to receive a balancing allowance when the asset is sold, thereby accelerating the allowances.
When not to elect?	Do not elect if expect to sell for more than tax written down value – this will give rise to a balancing charge. This will be the case if AIA is claimed.
What if not sold?	If not sold within eight years of the end of the period in which acquired, the asset's TWDV will be transferred into the main pool at the start of the following period.

Structures and buildings allowances (SBA)

Available on construction or renovation of a building on or after 6 April 2020 in the FTX exam.

On acquisition

- A separate capital allowance for commercial structures and buildings only.
- Each building is treated separately – include conversion/renovation costs, but exclude land, legal fees and planning permission.
- Calculation of SBAs:
  - 3% p.a. straight line on cost
  - from date first brought into use
  - time apportion for short/long periods.

On disposal

- Seller time apportions SBAs to date of disposal.
- No balancing allowance or balancing charge.
- Sale proceeds for calculation of gain = increased by SBAs claimed.
- Buyer receives remainder of SBAs at 3% based on original cost.

chapter

3

Trading losses and taxation of partnerships

In this chapter

- Trading losses.
- Partnerships.
- Taxation of partners.

Trading losses

Trading losses

- Calculated in the same way as a trading profit.
- Trading income is nil.

Relief against total income

- Available in:
  - – tax year of the loss and/or,
  - – preceding tax year

Choice available to relieve total income of:

- year of loss then previous year
- previous year first then year of loss
- year of loss only
- previous year only

- Offset cannot be restricted to preserve PA (no partial claims).
- Excess loss is automatically carried forward.

Relief against future trading profits

- Relieved against:
  - – the first available
  - – trading profits only
  - – of the same trade.
- Loss offset cannot be restricted.

Which relief should you choose?

- Try to save tax at 40%/45% rather than 20%.
- Try to avoid wasting the personal allowance (PA) and the savings and dividend nil rate bands, resulting in a tax saving at 0%.
- Try to relieve loss as soon as possible.

Income tax loss pro forma

This pro forma assumes a loss is incurred in 2025/26 which fully covers all income for 2025/26 and 2024/25 with a balance carried forward to 2026/27. It demonstrates where the losses are deducted in the computation.

	2024/25 Previous tax year	2025/26 Year of loss	2026/27
	£	£	£
Trade profits	X	0	X
Less: Trading loss b/f			(X)
			X
Employment income	X	X	X
Savings income	X	X	X
Dividend income	X	X	X
Total income	X	X	X
Less: Loss relief	(X)	(X)	–
Net income	0	0	X
Less: Personal allowance	Not used	Not used	(X)
Taxable income	0	0	X

Claims made 'as early as possible'

If an examination question states that losses should be claimed as early as possible:

- claim in prior year first, then
- claim in current year if there is sufficient loss.

Do this regardless of whether it wastes the PA.

Chargeable gains

For FTX: trading loss claims against chargeable gains will not be made.

Note: Do not combine gains with income for individuals

– they are always dealt with separately.

Partnerships

Treat like sole traders – each partner is the owner of the business.

Step 1	Calculate capital allowances for the partnership's period of account (for cars only if cash basis).
Step 2	Calculate partnership's taxable trading profits under cash basis (or accruals, if elected), deducting capital allowances.
Step 3	Allocate these profits between the partners according to the **profit sharing agreement** (PSA) in the **period of account**. If PSA requires a salary or interest on capital allocation: • treat as a share in their trading profits (these are **not** partnership expenses). The balance of profits or losses: • shared in the profit sharing ratio (PSR). **If a partner joins or leaves during the accounting period:** • treat as if a change in PSR • time apportion profits (and salaries and interest), apply appropriate PSA to each part.
Step 4	Allocate each partner's share of profit to a tax year(s), applying tax year basis rules for each partner individually.

e.g

Example

Troy and Paris have been in partnership for many years preparing accounts to 31 March. In the year ended 31 March 2026 the partnership has £60,000 taxable profits.

Until 30 September 2025 they share profits equally but from that date they start to pay an annual salary of £10,000 to Troy and share the balance of profits 30% for Troy and 70% for Paris.

The profit allocation for the year ended 31 March 2026 will be:

	Total	Troy	Paris
	£	£	£
1 April 2025 – 30 September 2025			
6/12 × £60,000 = £30,000 shared (1:1)	30,000	15,000	15,000
1 October 2025 – 31 March 2026			
Salary (6/12 × £10,000)	5,000	5,000	–
Balance (£30,000 – £5,000) = £25,000 Shared (30:70)	25,000	7,500	17,500
Total allocation	60,000	27,500	32,500

Taxation of partners

- The partnership itself is not taxed.
- Instead, each partner is
  - treated as a sole trader
  - taxed on that partner's share of the profits.

chapter

4

Income tax computations

In this chapter

- Tax year.
- Taxable income.
- Exempt income.
- Income tax computation.
- Pro forma – income tax computation.
- Calculation of income tax payable.
- Reliefs.
- Personal allowance.
- Dividends.
- Savings income.
- Property income.

Tax year

- An individual's taxable income is taxed in respect of a tax year
- Runs from 6 April to following 5 April
- Tax year 2025/26: 6 April 2025 to 5 April 2026

Taxable income

Income taxable	Basis of assessment
Profits from trade/profession	Tax year basis - Chapter 1
Interest received from UK sources Income from employment Dividend income	Income received in the tax year (gross)
Property income	Rental profits received in the tax year

Exempt income

Not taxable – do not include in calculation of taxable income

Includes:

- Premium Bond prizes
- Betting/gambling winnings
- Returns on NS&I savings certificates
- Income (interest and dividends) received from ISAs (individual savings accounts).

Exam focus

If exempt income appears in an examination question then put a note at the bottom of the income tax computation stating that it is exempt so the examining team know you have not just ignored it.

Income tax computation

Exam focus

Income tax will always be tested in one of the 15 mark questions in Part B, with an income tax computation likely to be required.

Income taxed at different rates depending on type of income:

Non-savings	Savings	Dividends
Employment income Trading profits Property income	Interest	Dividends

Exam focus

Use the following income tax pro forma to make sure that income tax is calculated at the correct rates on different sources of income.

Pro forma – Income tax computation – 2025/26

	Non-savings	Savings	Dividends	Total
	£	£	£	£
Employment income	X			X
Trading profits	X			X
Transition profits	X			X
Property income	X			X
Interest received		X		X
Dividends received			X	X
	———	———	———	———
Total income	X	X	X	X
Less: Reliefs	(X)			(X)
	———	———	———	———
Net income	X	X	X	X
Less: Personal allowance (PA)	(12,570)			(12,570)
	———	———	———	———
Taxable income	X	X	X	X
	———	———	———	———

Calculation of income tax payable

		£
Non-savings income		
On first £37,700	× 20%	X
£37,701 – £125,140	× 40%	X
£125,141 +	× 45%	X
		X
Savings income	× 0/20/40/45%	X
Dividend income	× 0/8.75/33.75/39.35%	X
Income tax liability		X
Less: PAYE		(X)
Income tax payable		X

Key Point

Income tax rate bands apply to the different types of income in the following order:

(1) non-savings income

(2) savings income

(3) dividend income.

Key Point

The gross amounts of gift aid payments and contributions to personal pension schemes should be used to increase the higher (40%) and additional (45%) rate thresholds.

Reliefs

- Are an allowable deduction from total income.
- Main examples
  - Qualifying interest e.g. interest on loans to purchase plant and machinery for use in an employment, interest on loans to allow a partner to purchase a share in a partnership or contribute capital/loan to the partnership.
  - Trading losses.

Personal allowance

- Available to all individuals.
- £12,570 for 2025/26.
- Deducted from net income to give taxable income.
- Not transferable in FTX syllabus.
- Lost if not used in the year.

Reduction in PA

If adjusted net income exceeds £100,000 then PA reduced as follows:

	£	£
PA		12,570
Net income	X	
Less: Gross gift aid contributions	(X)	
Gross personal pension scheme contributions	(X)	
Adjusted net income	A	
Less: Limit	(100,000)	
	B	
50% of B		(X)
Reduced PA (minimum £Nil)		X

Dividends

- Dividends are taxed as follows:

Nil rate band	0%
Basic rate band	8.75%
Higher rate band	33.75%
Additional rate	39.35%

- Dividend nil rate band: £500 for all taxpayers.

Savings income

- Savings income includes all interest received.
- Main examples of taxable interest income:
  - Interest from banks and building societies
  - Interest on NS&I savings accounts
  - Interest from Government Stocks (gilts).

Remember that

- interest from ISAs and returns on NS&I savings certificates are exempt
- savings income falling in the first £5,000 of taxable income is charged at 0%
- Rates of tax:

Basic rate (First £37,700) (Note)	20%
Higher rate (£37,701 – £125,140)	40%
Additional rate (£125,141 and over)	45%
Savings income nil rate band:	
– Basic rate taxpayers	£1,000
– Higher rate taxpayers	£500

Note: 0% starting rate where savings income falls within first £5,000 of taxable income.

Property income

Income	• Compute using **cash basis** (i.e. rental income actually received in the tax year less expenses actually paid) • Taxpayer can elect to use **accruals basis** and must use it if rents exceed £150,000 (i.e. rent due in the tax year less expenses payable) Chapter 10 explains how to calculate property income under the accruals basis • Always use cash basis in the exam unless told otherwise
Premium	Taxed in year of receipt. Calculated using the formula: Premium — £ X Less: Premium × 2% × (no. of years of lease – 1) — (X) Taxable — X

Expenses	• Wholly and exclusively test • Interest on loan to buy property is deductible (not examinable re residential property) • Capital purchases are generally deductible when paid except: – new assets for use in a residential property, e.g. furniture, TV, carpets, etc. Replacement of domestic items relief may be available (see below) – cars – land and buildings • Replacement of domestic items relief – deduction for replacement cost of similar item less any disposal proceeds • Capital allowances are available on cars (Chapter 2) or a flat rate expense deduction for motor expenses can be claimed instead using the AMAP rates (Chapter 5)
Private use	Apportion expenses based on the amount of time the property is available for letting
Tax rates	Taxed as non-savings income at 20%, 40% or 45%
Losses	Losses for individuals can only be carried forward against future property income

Rent-a-room relief

- Furnished room in a main domestic residence.
- Gross rents ≤ £7,500 are exempt.
- Two options for gross rents > £7,500
  - normal calculation, or
  - elect for excess over £7,500 to be taxed (with no relief for expenses).

Exam focus

You are given the figure of £7,500 in the examination.

chapter

5

Employment income

In this chapter

- Basis of assessment.
- Allowable expenses.
- Approved mileage allowances.
- Exempt benefits.
- Benefits.
- Accommodation.
- Cars and car fuel.
- Vans and van fuel.
- Beneficial loans.
- Use of assets.
- Gift of assets.
- PAYE forms.

Basis of assessment

Basis of assessment

Receipts basis:

Earnings are treated as received on the earlier of:

- actual payment, or
- becoming entitled to payment.

Directors – earliest of the above and:

- when credited in the accounts
- the end of the period of account, if earnings determined before then
- the date the earnings are determined, if after the end of the period of account.

Employment income pro forma

	£
Salary/wages	X
Bonus	X
Benefits	X
	X
Less: Allowable deductions	(X)
Employment income	X

Income taxable

- Earnings from office or employment including:
  - salaries
  - wages
  - bonuses
  - benefits.

Allowable expenses

Allowable expenses

- Expenses incurred wholly, exclusively and necessarily in the performance of the duties.
- Travel expenses (but not home to work).
- Subscriptions to professional bodies.
- Contributions to an occupational pension scheme.
- Donations to charity under a payroll deduction scheme.

Approved mileage allowances

- Apply to employees using their own vehicle for business travel.

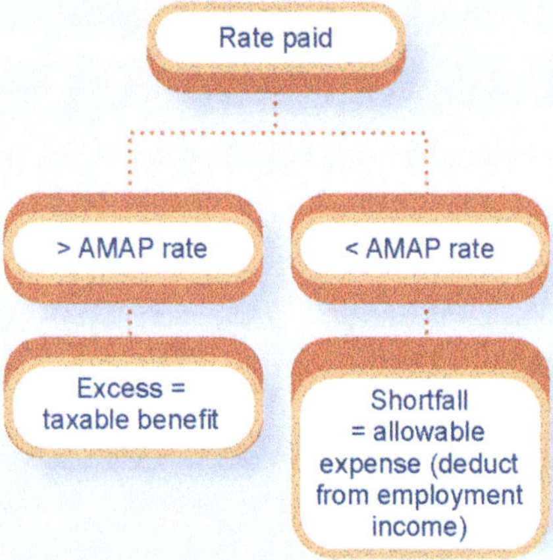

Use of car and van allowance

- Mileage allowances paid up to the following amounts are tax free:

Cars and vans	
First 10,000 business miles	45p a mil
Each additional mile	25p a mil

- These approved mileage allowances are provided in the tax tables available in the examination.

Passenger allowance

- Employers can also make tax free payments of up to 5p per mile per passenger.
- Where the passenger is also an employee travelling on business purposes (but employee cannot claim deduction if employer does not pay).

Exempt benefits

- Job-related accommodation (see later)
- Subsidised canteen
- Employer's pension contribution
- Workplace parking
- Removal expenses ≤ £8,000
- Overnight subsistence (£5 per night in UK, £10 overseas)
- Mobile phone (only one per employee)
- Workplace nurseries
- Annual party ≤ £150/head
- Loans totalling ≤ £10,000 throughout the year
- Medical treatment up to £500 per year for return to work
- Up to £6 a week towards household costs where employee works from home
- Pool cars
- Approved mileage allowances (see above)
- Long service awards, not in cash, up to £50 per year of service of 20 years +
- Recreational / sporting facilities available to employees generally and not the general public
- Trivial benefits no more than £50 per gift per employee (not cash or vouchers and not provided in recognition of services provided)
- Staff uniforms and protective clothing for work purposes.

Benefits

- General rule:

  Taxed on cost to employer, i.e. additional/marginal cost.

- Special rules for:

  Cars, car fuel, vans, beneficial loans, use and gift of assets and accommodation (see below).

- Rules applicable to all taxable benefits
  - Reduced by contributions made by the employee towards the cost (exception for private fuel).
  - Time apportioned if only available for part of the tax year.

Accommodation

Benefit	Amount taxable
Basic charge	Higher of: (i) the annual value and (ii) rent paid by employer
Additional charge where property cost more than £75,000	(Cost (Note) – £75,000) × official rate of interest at start of tax year
Ancillary services (a) Use of furniture (b) Living expenses e.g. lighting/heating, cleaning, decorating	(a) 20% of market value when first provided (b) Cost to employer
Note: Cost = Acquisition cost plus improvement costs up to start of tax year. Substitute MV at time first occupied by employee if the employer has owned the property for over six years before the employee moved in.	

Exam focus

You need to remember the additional charge figure of £75,000 as you will not be given it in the examination.

Job-related accommodation

- Necessary for proper performance of employee's duties or,
- Provided for better performance of duties and it is customary to provide such accommodation or,
- Provided as part of special security arrangements because of a specific threat to the employee's security.

Consequences

Benefit	Amount taxable
Basic charge	Exempt
Additional charge	Exempt
Ancillary services	As for non job-related accommodation but maximum benefit restricted to 10% of other employment income

Cars and car fuel

The charge	List price × %
List price	The price published by the manufacturer at the date of the car's first registration. Not the price actually paid by the employer.
Additions	The cost of any accessories paid for by the employer is added to the list price.
The %	51 – 54g/km = 16% 55g/km = 17% Increased by 1% for each complete 5 grams of CO_2 above 55. Maximum 37%
Diesel cars	Attract a 4% surcharge unless car meets the RDE2 standards (will be stated in question). Maximum still 37%.
Hybrid-electric and electric cars	Zero emission cars are taxed at 3% For cars that emit between 1 and 50g/km, percentage depends on the electric range of the car. ≥130 miles 3% 70–129 miles 6% 40–69 miles 9% 30–39 miles 13% <30 miles 15%

Fuel	£28,200 × same %
Contributions	• **Capital** = contribution towards the cost of the car. Reduces the list price of the car. Maximum reduction £5,000. • **For private use of car** = £ for £ reduction in the benefit charge. • **For private fuel** = no reduction in fuel benefit. Must repay cost of all private fuel in order to avoid fuel benefit.
Tax tables	In the examination you are provided with the above figures apart from the diesel supplement for cars that do not meet the RDE2 standard, the maximum percentage and the cap of £5,000 for capital contributions.

Example

Daphne is employed by Z Ltd. On 1 June 2025 she was provided with a diesel car which cost £15,000. The car does not meet the RDE2 standards. It has CO_2 emissions of 102g/km and had a list price when new of £19,000.

Z Ltd paid insurance of £850, repair costs of £400 and fuel costs of £2,500 in 2025/26.

Daphne uses the car 80% for business purposes and contributes £250 p.a. for private fuel.

Taxable benefits for 2025/26:		£
Car	(£19,000 × 30% × 10/12)	4,750
Private fuel	(£28,200 × 30% × 10/12)	7,050
Total benefit		11,800

Notes:

- Appropriate percentage = (100 – 55) ÷ 5 = (9% + 17% + 4%) = 30%
- Only available for 10 months of the year
- Diesel engine = 4% supplement
- No deduction for contribution to fuel as cost not fully reimbursed
- Cost to Z Ltd of car is irrelevant
- Car benefit covers all costs incurred except private fuel.

Vans and van fuel

These figures are provided in the tax tables in the examination.

Beneficial loans

- Interest free/subsidised loan made to employee.
- Benefit:

	£
Capital × official rate of interest	X
Less: Interest actually paid	(X)
Taxable benefit	X

- Two methods of computation:

(1) Average method:

$$\frac{\text{Opening balance} + \text{Closing balance}}{2} = \text{Average capital}$$

(2) Precise method:

calculated day by day on balance outstanding (calculate to nearest month in examination).

- Either taxpayer or HMRC can elect for precise method to be used.
- No benefit where loan is ≤ £10,000 throughout the year.

Exam focus

You are provided with the official rate of interest in the examination.

Use of assets

- Benefit = 20% × MV when first made available.
- 20% rule does not apply to private use of cars, vans and accommodation.
- Can deduct % business use.

Gift of assets

- New asset: benefit = cost to employer
- Used asset compare:

	£	£	£
MV at date gifted		A	
MV when first made available	X		
Less: Benefits taxed on employee for use of asset	(X)		
		B	
Higher of A and B			X
Less: Payment by employee			(X)
Taxable benefit			X

- Exception:

  Cars are taxed on the MV at date of gift, less any payment by employee.

PAYE forms

Number	Purpose	Submit by?
P11D	Provides details of deductible expenses and taxable benefits for directors and employees	6 July
P60	End of year summary for employee showing pay, tax and NICs for the year	31 May
P45	Details an employee's pay and tax for that year up to the date of employee leaving	–

Under the Real Time Information system, employers submit details of pay, tax and NICs monthly to HMRC for all employees.

Exam focus

- The calculation of employment income, particularly the benefit rules, is likely to be tested in every exam.

chapter

6

National insurance and pensions

In this chapter

- National insurance for the self-employed.
- National insurance for employees.
- National insurance for employers.
- Pension contributions.

National insurance for the self-employed

Key Point

The self-employed pay class 4 contributions if aged between 16 and state pension age.

Class 4

- The rate of 6% applies to 'profits', defined as:

	£
Trading profits	X
Less: Trading losses	(X)
	X

- There are no class 4 contributions payable on profits up to £12,570.
- Liability at the rate of 6% applies only to profits in the range £12,570 to £50,270.
- Profits above £50,270 are charged at the rate of 2%.
- Class 4 contributions are usually collected with the income tax liability under the self-assessment system.

National insurance for employees

Key Point

Class 1 employee contributions are paid by employees aged between 16 and state pension age.

- It is paid on 'earnings' which include salary, bonus and vouchers, but not benefits.
- Employee contributions are not payable on earnings up to £12,570.
- Employee contributions are payable at 8% on earnings in the range £12,570 to £50,270.
- Earnings above the upper threshold are charged at the rate of 2%.
- Contributions are calculated on a weekly or monthly basis according to when an employee is paid.
- Each pay date is looked at in isolation.

e.g

Example

June is paid a salary of £250 a week. She was also paid a bonus of £10,000 in the last week of March 2026. The upper and lower weekly thresholds for employee's class 1 are £242 and £967 respectively.

NICs due:

		£
(£250 – £242)	× 51 × 8%	33
(£967 – £242)	× 1 × 8%	58
(£10,250 – £967)	× 1 × 2%	186
		277

National insurance for employers

Class 1

- Paid in respect of employees aged 16 and over.
- Employer's contributions are payable at 15% by employers on all earnings (i.e. salary and bonus) over the threshold of £5,000 p.a.
- There is no upper earnings threshold.
- The employer must pay both the employee and the employer's contributions to HMRC within 14 days of the end of each tax month (i.e. by 19th of the month or 22nd if paying electronically).

NIC employment allowance

- £10,500 relief per employer per tax year
- Offset against employer's class 1 NICs only.
- Claimed as part of normal payroll through RTI.

Class 1A

- Employers must also pay class 1A national insurance contributions where benefits are provided to an employee or director.
- Class 1A is paid at the rate of 15% on the benefit value as calculated for income tax purposes.
- Class 1A is due by 19 July following the end of the tax year or 22 July if paying electronically.

Pension contributions

Annual limit	• Contributions qualifying for relief are limited to a maximum of the higher of 100% of relevant earnings or £3,600 • However, contributions in excess of the annual allowance (£60,000 in 2025/26) are subject to a tax charge, which cancels out the tax relief given • The calculation of this tax charge is not examinable
Relevant earnings	• Employment income (including benefits) and trading income
How is relief given?	• Contributions to an occupational pension scheme are deducted from employment income • Contributions to a personal pension scheme are paid net of basic rate tax. Higher and additional rate relief is given by extending the tax rate thresholds by the gross contribution

chapter

7

Capital gains tax

In this chapter

- Scope of CGT.
- Order of computation – individuals.
- Chargeable gain computation pro forma – individuals.
- Tax rates.
- Part disposals.
- Chattels.
- How do companies differ?
- Chargeable gain computation pro forma – companies.

Scope of CGT

Chargeable gains

A chargeable gain arises when

- a chargeable disposal is made
- of a chargeable asset
- by a chargeable person.

Tax payable

Individuals = Capital gains tax

Companies = Corporation tax

Chargeable gains

Chargeable persons

- individual
- company

Chargeable assets

- all assets unless specifically exempt

Chargeable disposals

- sale
- gift
- exchange
- loss/destruction of asset
- compensation for damage

Exempt assets

Examples:

- cars
- non-wasting chattels bought & sold for <£6,000
- cash
- wasting chattels (e.g. horses, boats, caravan)
- qualifying corporate bonds (QCBs) owned by individuals
- individual's private residence (if occupied for full ownership period)
- assets held in ISAs

Exempt disposals

- transfers on death
- transfers to charity

Order of computation – individuals

- Compute the gain/loss for each individual capital transaction separately
- Apply any available reliefs (e.g. rollover relief, gift holdover relief, PRR)
- Deduct any current year allowable capital losses
- Aggregate the chargeable gains (after reliefs) on the individual assets
- Deduct the annual exempt amount (£3,000 for 2025/26 cannot be carried forward or back)
- Deduct any brought forward capital losses
- Calculate CGT at appropriate rate depending on level of taxable income, and whether BADR claimed
- Pay by 31 January following end of tax year

Chargeable gain computation pro forma – individuals

	£	£	Notes
Disposal proceeds		X	Use market value (MV) if gifted
Less: Incidental costs of sale		(X)	(e.g. legal expenses, auctioneer's fees, etc.)
Net sale proceeds		NSP	
Less: Allowable expenditure			
– acquisition cost	X		Use MV if gift or probate value if inherited
– incidental costs of acquisition	X		(e.g. surveyor's fees, stamp duties, etc.)
– enhancement expenditure	X		(i.e. improvements)
		(Cost)	
Chargeable gain/Allowable loss		X/(X)	

Tax rates

- Rate of tax on capital gains is dependent on an individual's taxable income, and the availability of business asset disposal relief.
- Where an individual is already paying income tax at 40% or more, then capital gains are charged at the higher rate.
- Where a taxpayer has taxable income falling below the basic rate threshold then the gains equal to the difference between the taxable income and the basic rate threshold are taxed at the lower rate, and the balance at the higher rate.
- If the gain qualifies for business asset disposal relief the gain is taxed at 14% irrespective of the level of taxable income.
- Rates of tax:

Lower rate	18%
Higher rate	24%

- Allowable capital losses and the annual exempt amount should be deducted first from gains not qualifying for business asset disposal relief before gains qualifying for the relief.

e.g

Example

Jatinder has taxable income of £32,500 and taxable gains of £13,000 for 2025/26.

Capital gains tax payable:

£		£
5,200*	at 18%	936
7,800	at 24%	1,872
13,000		
CGT payable		2,808

* Balance of basic rate band is (£37,700 – £32,500) = £5,200

- Gains qualifying for business asset disposal relief are deemed to use up the basic rate band first.

Payment of tax on residential property

- A return must be submitted within 60 days of disposal with CGT payable on gain (unless PRR covers gain).
- CGT paid is deducted from final payment due on 31 January following tax year.

Part disposals

Key Point

Where only part of an asset is disposed of, the original cost is adjusted to reflect the cost of the part sold.

- Cost of part of asset disposed of:

$$\text{Original cost} \times \frac{A}{A + B}$$

Where:

A = consideration
B = MV of the remainder

- Incidental costs which relate wholly to the part sold are fully deductible
- Cost of the part retained:

	£
Original cost	x
Less: Cost of part disposed of (as above)	(x)
	x

e.g

Example

Albert purchased 36 hectares of land for £210,000. He sold 10 hectares for £150,000. The value of the remaining 26 hectares was £300,000.

When computing the gain arising on the part disposal, the allowable cost is:

$$£210,000 \times \frac{£150,000}{£150,000 + £300,000} = £70,000$$

The cost of the part retained is:
(£210,000 – £70,000) = £140,000

Chattels

Definition

Chattel: Tangible movable property (i.e. not land, shares)

Wasting chattel: expected life ≤ 50 years (e.g. dog)

Non-wasting chattel: expected life > 50 years (e.g. antique furniture, painting)

- Special rules apply to non-wasting chattels:

Gross Sales proceeds \ Cost	£6,000 or less	More than £6,000
£6,000 or less	Exempt	Allowable loss based on deemed **gross** sales proceeds of £6,000
More than £6,000	Normal computation but gain is restricted to: 5/3 x (**gross** proceeds – £6,000)	Normal gain computation

Key Point

Wasting chattels are exempt assets.

e.g

Example

Beth sold an antique table for £6,800 (after auctioneer's costs of £200). The table cost £4,500.

Beth's capital gain under the normal CGT rules would be £2,300 (£6,800 – £4,500).

However, as the table is a chattel, the gain is restricted to:

5/3 × (£7,000 – £6,000) = £1,667.

Note: In the 5/3 formula you must use the gross sales proceeds (i.e. add back selling costs of £200 to £6,800 net sale proceeds).

Chattels with capital allowances

- Sold for more than original cost: calculate gain as normal.
- Sold for less than original cost: no chargeable gain or allowable loss.

Exam focus

The chattels rules are frequently examined.

Assets lost or destroyed

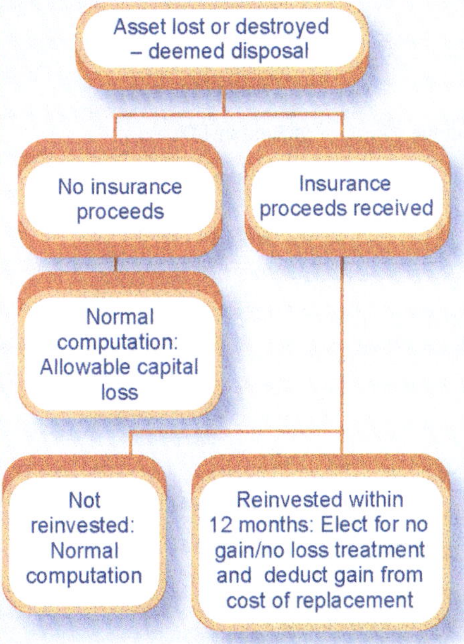

How do companies differ?

	Individuals	Companies
Gains subject to	Capital gains tax – tax separately from income	Corporation tax – include in TTP – tax with income
Taxable period	Tax year	Accounting period
Annual exempt amount (AEA)	✓	✗
Indexation allowance	✗	✓ (up to December 2017)
Treatment of capital losses	• Current year offset – before AEA which may be wasted • Carry forward – after AEA	• Current year offset in full • Carry forward in full

Chargeable gain computation pro forma – companies

	£	£	Notes
Disposal proceeds		X	Use market value (MV) if gifted
Less: Incidental costs of sale		(X)	(e.g. legal expenses, auctioneer's fees)
Net sale proceeds		NSP	
Less: Allowable expenditure			
– acquisition cost	X		Use MV if was gifted
– incidental costs of acquisition	X		(e.g. surveyor's fees, stamp duty, etc.)
– enhancement expenditure	X		(i.e. improvements)
		(Cost)	
Unindexed gain/loss		X/(X)	
Less: Indexation allowance			Cannot increase/create a loss
= 0.XXX × Cost (Note)		(IA)	Index enhancement costs separately
Chargeable gain/allowable loss		X/(X)	

Note: Indexation factor will be provided in the question and runs from acquisition up to date of sale or December 2017 if earlier.

chapter

8

CGT – Reliefs

In this chapter

- Types of relief.
- Private residence relief (PRR).
- Business asset disposal relief.
- Rollover relief (replacement of business assets).
- Reinvestment in depreciating assets.
- Gift holdover relief.

Types of relief

Types of relief		
Permanent reliefs	**Deferral reliefs**	**Reduction in tax rate**
Private residence relief	Rollover relief Gift holdover relief	Business asset disposal relief
Gain never becomes chargeable	Gain remains chargeable, but deferred to later date	Eligible gain is only taxable at 14% regardless of level of income

Key Point

Rollover relief is the only relief available to companies.

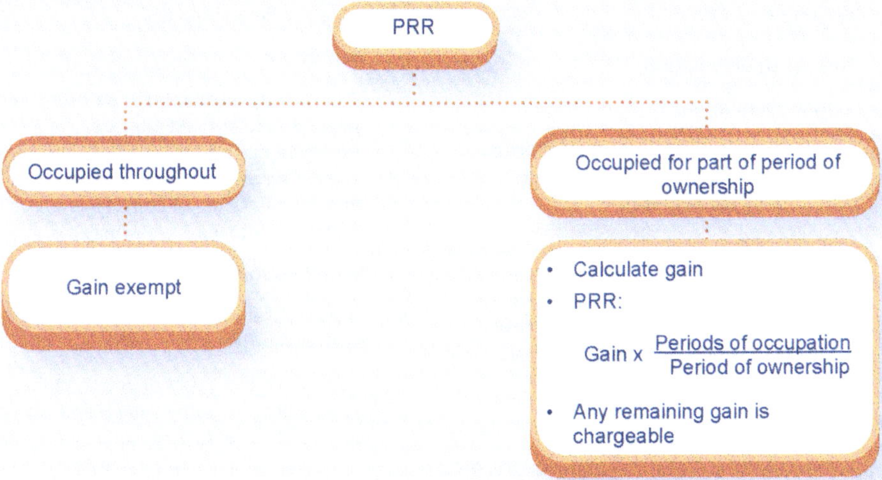

Exam focus

The examining team may require you to calculate the relief, or may require you to explain the rules and identify periods of deemed occupation.

Private residence relief (PRR)

Periods of occupation

Actual occupation:

Any period in which the property is actually occupied as the only, or main, private residence by the taxpayer.

Deemed occupation:

Final nine months of ownership

Always count as a period of occupation, even if the taxpayer was absent or has moved to a new PR.

Conditional periods

These are periods in which the taxpayer was absent from the property, but which are still counted as periods of occupation:

- up to three years absence for any reason
- any period spent working abroad
- up to four years absence working elsewhere in the UK.

Condition:

The property must actually be occupied before and after these periods
(unless re occupation was prevented after working abroad or elsewhere in the UK because the terms of employment required the taxpayer to work elsewhere).

More than one residence:

The taxpayer can choose which property to treat as the PR.

Elect within two years of acquiring the second property, otherwise HMRC decides as a question of fact.

Business asset disposal relief

Available to	Individuals only
Operation of the relief	• First £1 million of gains on qualifying business disposals are taxed at 14% • All gains above the £1 million limit taxed at usual rates • £1 million is a lifetime limit
Qualifying disposals	• Disposal of the whole or part of business carried on by sole trader • Disposal of shares in individual's 'personal trading company', provided the individual is an employee of the company (full-time or part-time)
Qualifying ownership period	• 2 years prior to disposal • For shares, the individual must be employed ≥ 2 years

Note: The disposal of an individual business asset used for the purposes of a continuing trade **does not qualify.**

A 'personal trading company' = broadly where the individual owns ≥ 5% of the ordinary shares.

Rollover relief (replacement of business assets)

Definition

Rollover relief

The gain on a qualifying asset used in a business can be deferred if its net sale proceeds are reinvested in qualifying replacement assets within the qualifying period.

Available to	Companies, sole traders and partnerships
Qualifying assets	Land & buildings, fixed plant & machinery and goodwill (unincorporated businesses only) – must be used in the trade
Qualifying period	From one year before to three years after the date of disposal
Reinvestment of full proceeds	The whole gain is deferred by deducting it from the cost of the replacement asset (unless reinvestment is in depreciating asset – see below)
Partial reinvestment	• Immediate charge on lower of (a) amount retained, and (b) amount of gain • Remaining gain deferred by deducting it from the cost of the replacement asset

Example

Selma sold a factory, which she used in her business, on 1 June 2025 for £250,000. The capital gain was £50,000.

Selma will purchase one of two new factories, A, costing £320,000 or B, costing £210,000 within the next year.

Factory A Cost = £320,000	Factory B Cost = £210,000
Proceeds fully reinvested Chargeable gain 2025/26: £0	Proceeds not reinvested £40,000 (£250,000 – £210,000) Chargeable gain 2025/26, lower of: (i) Total gain = £50,000 (ii) Amount not reinvested = £40,000 i.e. £40,000
Gain rolled over: £50,000	Gain rolled over: Total gain less amount chargeable now = (£50,000 – £40,000) = £10,000
CGT base cost of Factory A: £ Cost 320,000 Less: Gain rolled over (50,000) Base cost 270,000	CGT base cost of Factory B: £ Cost 210,000 Less: Gain rolled over (10,000) Base cost 200,000

Reinvestment in depreciating assets

Definition

Rollover relief is modified where the replacement asset is classed as a depreciating asset.

Depreciating asset (DA):

Life of ≤ 50 years or will be DA within 10 years.

Examples of DAs

Fixed plant and machinery, leases of no more than 60 years.

Key Point

- Conditions as for non-depreciating assets.
- Gain not deducted from base cost of new asset.
- Gain is held over and crystallises (becomes chargeable) on the earliest of:
  - sale of DA
  - date DA ceases to be used in trade
  - 10 years from acquisition of DA.

Gift holdover relief (Gift relief)

Available to	• Individuals only
Operation of the relief	• Gift is treated as sale at market value • Donee is treated as acquiring asset at market value • Donor's gain is deducted from the MV of the asset acquired by donee (i.e. donee effectively acquires asset for donor's base cost)
Qualifying assets	• Assets used in trade of donor or the donor's personal company • Shares in unquoted trading company • Shares in donor's personal trading company (owns ≥ 5% voting rights)
Sales at under value	• Asset sold at less than MV • Where sale proceeds exceed original cost, excess is chargeable immediately • The excess may qualify for business asset disposal relief and be taxed at 14%
Restriction re shares	• For shares (if own ≥ 5% voting rights) proportion of gain qualifying for relief is: $\frac{\text{MV Chargeable business assets}}{\text{MV Chargeable assets}} \times \text{gains}$ • Chargeable assets = Any asset chargeable to CGT on disposal • Chargeable business assets = Chargeable assets excluding investments

Exam focus

Gift holdover relief is available on gifts by individuals only.

chapter

9

CGT – Shares and securities

In this chapter

- Valuation rules.
- Matching rules – individuals.
- Matching rules – companies.
- The share pool for companies.
- Bonus issues.
- Rights issues.

Valuation rules

Transaction:	Consideration:
Sale	Sale proceeds
Gift	Market value

Market value of quoted shares:

- Average of highest and lowest closing prices = (highest + lowest) x ½.

Matching rules – individuals

Apply where an individual has made more than one purchase of shares of the same class in the same company. Disposals matched in the following order:

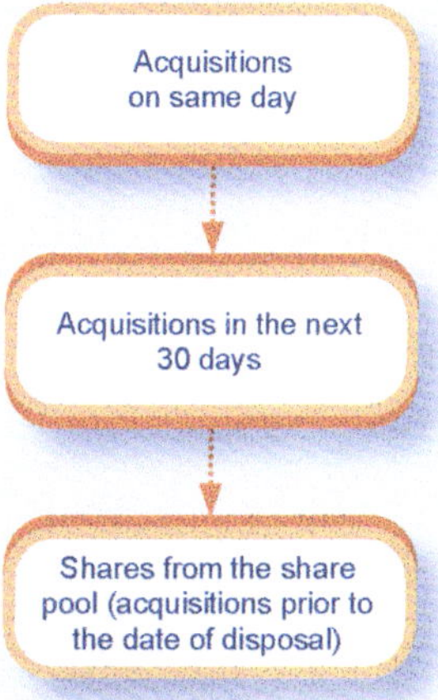

Example

Ethel sold 1,200 shares in Red plc on 1 August 2025. She made purchases of the shares as follows:

500 on 1 April 1986, 800 on 1 May 1988, 200 on 1 June 2001 and 300 on 15 August 2025.

The disposal will be matched with:

(1) 300 acquired on 15 August 2025;

(2) 900 out of the pool of 1,500 shares acquired prior to 1 August 2025.

Key Point

Ethel will have two separate CGT computations (i.e. one for each category of disposal).

The pool operates as follows:

	No. of shares	Cost
		£
Purchase	X	X
Purchase	X	X
Purchase	X	X
	X	X
Disposal	(X)	(X)*
Balance c/f	X	X

*Where shares are disposed of from the pool, a proportion of the cost should be removed from the pool.

This will be used to calculate the capital gain on disposal.

$$\frac{\text{Number of shares sold}}{\text{Number of shares in pool}} \times \text{Cost to date}$$

Matching rules – companies

The share pool for companies

- Identifies cost and indexation allowance of shares acquired.
- Records the number of shares held, the unindexed cost and the indexed cost.
- Indexation is added to the pool before each 'operative event' (i.e. purchase, sale, rights issue), up to December 2017.

Pro forma for share pool for companies

	Number of shares	Cost	Indexed cost
		£	£
Purchase	X	X	X
Index to next operative event*			X
Purchase	X	X	X
	X	X	X
Index to next operative event*			X
	X	X	X
Sale	(X)	(X) W1	(X) W2
Pool carried forward	X	X	X

*An operative event is a purchase, rights issue or sale of shares.

W1 $\frac{\text{Number of shares sold}}{\text{Number of shares in pool}}$ x Cost to date

W2 $\frac{\text{Number of shares sold}}{\text{Number of shares in pool}}$ x Indexed Cost to date

Final stage

	£
Sale proceeds	X
Less: Cost (W1)	(X)
Unindexed gain	X
Less: Indexation (W2 – W1)	(X)
Chargeable gain	X

Bonus issues

- A bonus issue = distribution of free shares to existing shareholders based on the number of shares owned.
- On a 1:4 bonus issue a shareholder with 400 shares would receive 100 free shares.

For capital gains purposes they are treated as follows:

- The bonus shares are not treated as a separate holding of shares.
- The shares are treated as acquired on the same day as the original shares to which they relate.
- Therefore, the number of bonus shares are included in the share pool but at Nil cost.

Rights issues

- A rights issue = a distribution of shares, normally at less than market value, to existing shareholders based on the number of shares owned.
- On a 1:3 rights issue at £10 per share, a shareholder with 300 shares would acquire 100 shares at a cost of £1,000.

For capital gains purposes they are treated as follows:

- The rights shares are not treated as a separate holding of shares.
- For matching purposes the shares are treated as acquired on the same day as the original shares to which they relate.
- For company share pools, the rights issue is indexed from the date actually acquired.
- Therefore, rights shares are included in the share pool in the same way as a normal purchase.

chapter

10

Corporation tax

In this chapter

- Pro forma corporation tax computation.
- Accounting periods (AP).
- Long period of account.
- Differences between companies and individuals.
- Enhanced capital allowances – additions.
- Enhanced capital allowances – disposals.
- Capital allowances pro forma for companies.
- Interest (loan relationships).
- Property income.
- Corporation tax liability.
- Loss relief for companies.

Pro forma corporation tax computation

XYZ Ltd – CT computation for period ended ....

	£
Tax adjusted trading profits (adjusted profit less CAs)	X
Interest income (see below)	X
Property business profits	X
Chargeable gains (net of any allowable losses)	X
Total profits	X
Less: Qualifying charitable donations (QCD) relief (paid gross)	(X)
Taxable total profits (TTP)	X

Exam focus

Qualifying charitable donations (QCDs) include all donations to charity by a company (excluding those allowed as a trading expense).

Dividends received by a company are **not** taxable income.

Accounting periods (AP)

Start	End
• When company starts to trade • When previous AP ends	• 12 months after start • At end of period of account (i.e. period for which company draws up accounts) • When cease to trade/be resident in UK • When go into administration/liquidation

Exam focus

Trading profits

If the exam question gives you:	
• Trading income, or • Adjusted trading profits	No further adjustment required
• Adjusted trading profits before	Further adjustment required

Long period of account

Key Point

If the period of account exceeds 12 months, the rules for splitting this period are:

1st AP = first 12 months of period of account

2nd AP = balance of months of the period of account

Allocate income between the two periods as follows:

Adjusted trading profit	Time apportion, before CAs
Capital allowances	Calculate separately for each AP
Property business profits	Accruals basis (time apportion if insufficient information)
Interest income	Accruals basis
Chargeable gains	Date of sale
QCD relief	Date of payment

Two corporation tax computations:

- Separate computation required for each AP
- Due dates = nine months and one day after the end of each AP (unless instalments are payable, see Chapter 13)
- One filing date = 12 months after the end of the period of account

Differences between companies and individuals

Companies	Individuals
Charged CT on profits and gains arising in an accounting period	Charged IT on income arising in a tax year and CGT on gains on disposals in a tax year
No personal allowance	Personal allowance
Trading income and CAs – accruals basis – no private use adjustments – enhanced capital allowances (see below)	Trading income and CAs – cash basis, unless elect for accruals basis – private expenditure by owner disallowed
Interest is dealt with on an accruals basis	Interest is dealt with on a receipts basis
Dividends received from other companies are not charged to CT	Dividends received from UK companies are chargeable to IT
Property income is calculated on the accruals basis	Property income is calculated on the cash basis unless taxpayer elects for the accruals basis or rents received exceed £150,000
Interest paid on loans to purchase let property is deducted from interest income	Interest paid on loans to purchase let property is dealt with under property income rules
QCDs are paid gross and are deducted in computing taxable total profits	Gift aid payments are paid net of basic rate tax. They are not deducted in computing taxable income. The gross amount increases the basic and higher rate limits

Enhanced capital allowances – additions

Companies can claim enhanced capital allowances when they purchase new plant and machinery.

- 100% first year allowance (FYA) for main pool expenditure (full expensing)
- 50% FYA for special rate pool (SRP) expenditure.

The relief is not available for

- cars
- second-hand assets
- assets purchased during the final accounting period of trading.

If there is only qualifying SRP expenditure in a period:

- first claim the AIA (max £1 million)
- then claim 50% FYA on remaining cost
- then transfer the balance to SRP, below the WDA, to c/f to next period.

If there are several additions, allocate AIA in order:

- second-hand assets
- new SRP expenditure
- new main pool expenditure

Exam focus

Between 1 April 2021 and 31 March 2023, companies were entitled to claim 130% for new additions of certain plant and machinery in the main pool (known as the super deduction).

In the examination, a question will not be set involving an initial claim for the 130% super deduction. However, you may be required to deal with the disposal of plant and machinery on which ECAs, including the super deduction, were claimed (see below).

Enhanced capital allowances – disposals

If **130% super deduction or 100% full expensing** was claimed:

- proceeds not deducted from pool
- balancing charge = proceeds

If **50% FYA** was claimed on **full cost**:

- balancing charge = 50% of proceeds
- 50% of proceeds deducted from SRP

If **50% FYA** was claimed on **part of cost**

- balancing charge = proceeds × proportion of cost on which FYA claimed × 50%
- remaining proceeds (i.e. proceeds – BC) deducted from SRP

Capital allowances pro forma for companies

	AIA	FYA	Full expense	Main pool	SRP	SLA	Allowances
	£	£	£	£	£	£	£
TWDV b/f				X	X	X	
Additions:							
Not qualifying for AIA/FYA:							
Second-hand zero-emission cars				X			
Cars (1 – 50g/km)				X			
Cars (over 50g/km)					X		
Qualifying for AIA:							
Second-hand SRP expenditure	X						
AIA (Max £1,000,000 in total)	(X)						X
Balance into the SRP (if any)					X		
Second-hand MP expenditure	X						
AIA (Max £1,000,000 in total)	(X)						X
Balance into the MP (if any)				X			
New SRP Additions	X						
AIA (Max £1,000,000 in total)	(X)						X
SRP Balance for 50% FYA (if any)		X					
New MP Additions	X						
AIA (Max £1,000,000 in total)	(X)						X
MP balance for full expensing			X				
Full expensing (100% FYA)			(X)				X

	AIA	FYA	Full expense	Main pool	SRP	SLA	Allowances
	£	£	£	£	£	£	£
Disposals							
BC for P&M on which ECA claimed (130%/100%)							(X)
BC on proceeds re 50% FYA							(X)
Remaining proceeds re 50% FYA					(X)		
All other disposals:							
(lower of original cost and proceeds)				(X)	(X)	(X)	
				X	X	X	
BA/BC						X/(X)	X/(X)
Small pool WDA (if applicable)							
WDA @ 18%				(X)			X
WDA @ 6%					(X)		X
Additions qualifying for FYAs:							
SRP with FYA 50%		(X)					X
Balance to SRP (WDA from next AP)					X		
Zero-emissions cars		X					
FYA @ 100%		(X)					X
				0			
TWDV c/f				X	X		
Total allowances							X

Interest (loan relationships)

	Trading loan	Non-trading loan
Examples	Loan notes issued to raise funds to acquire P&M Loan to purchase property used in trade e.g. office, warehouse, factory Overdraft financing working capital	Loan to acquire investment property or shares
Income (Note)	N/A	Interest income
Expense	Deduct from trading income	Deduct from interest income

Exam focus

Note: Interest received is always treated as non-trading interest income at FTX.

Property income

Property income for a company must be calculated on the **accruals basis** for the company's accounting period.

- Rental income and property expenses are taxable/deductible when they are due not when they are paid (as for trading profits).

The other differences from the rules for individuals are:

- Capital expenditure is not an allowable deduction for companies:
  - Capital allowances (see Chapter 2) may be claimed on plant and machinery (including cars) used for running the property business.
  - Replacement of domestic items relief is available re residential properties.
  - A company cannot use AMAP rates instead of capital allowances re motor expenses.
- Interest paid is not an expense of the property business, but deducted from interest received.
- Specific impaired debts are allowable, whilst a general allowance for impaired debts is not allowable.

Corporation tax liability

Financial year (FY)

The rates of tax are fixed for a FY.

FY runs from 1 April to 31 March, and is labelled by the calendar year in which it starts,
(e.g. 1 April 2025 – 31 March 2026 is FY2025).

Corporation tax rates

The corporation tax rate depends on a company's augmented profits.

Augmented profits are taxable total profits plus non-group dividends received.

- If augmented profits are equal to or above the upper limit of £250,000, the main rate of 25% applies.
- If augmented profits are equal to or below the lower limit of £50,000, the small profits rate of 19% applies.
- If augmented profits are between these limits, the main rate of 25% applies but tax is reduced by marginal relief (see later).

The limits are reduced for short accounting periods and for associated companies.

Exam focus

Accounting periods spanning two financial years where there has been a change in the rate of tax are not examinable.

Companies are associated with each other if either:

- one company controls the other, or
- they are both under common control.

Control = over 50% of the shares.

FY2025 CT summary

Augmented profits ≤ £50,000 (lower limit):
Corporation tax = Taxable total profits × 19%
Augmented profits ≥ £250,000 (upper limit)
Corporation tax = Taxable total profits × 25%
£50,000 < Augmented profits < £250,000

	£
Taxable total profits × 25% =	XX
Less Marginal relief:	
(Upper limit - Augmented Profits) × standard fraction × $\frac{\text{Taxable total profits}}{\text{Augmented profits}}$	(X)
Corporation tax liability	XX

The standard fraction for FY2025 is 3/200

Loss relief for companies

Type of loss	Carry back	Current period	Carry forward
Trading loss	Yes, but only after relief in current period	Against total profits before QCD relief	Against total profits before QCD relief (can choose amount to offset)
Capital loss	No	Against chargeable gains only	Against chargeable gains only
Loss on property business	No	Against total profits before QCD relief	Against total profits before QCD relief (can choose amount to offset)

Options for trading losses

Relief against total profits

- Set against total profits (before QCD relief) of the loss making accounting period, **then**
- Set against total profits (before QCD relief) of the previous 12 months (**optional**)
- Unrelieved QCD relief is wasted

Relief by carry forward

- Carry forward against total profits before QCD relief
- No time limit on carry forward
- Can choose amount to offset so QCD relief need not be wasted

Layout of corporation tax loss computation (loss in y/e 31 March 2026 for a continuing business)

y/e 31 March	2025	2026	2027
	£	£	£
Trading profits	X	0	X
Other income	X	X	X
Chargeable gains less allowable losses (Note i)	X	X	X
Total profits	X	X	X
Less: Loss relief – Current and carry back (Note ii)	(X)2	(X)1	–
Less: Loss relief b/f (Note iii)			(X)3
	0	0	X
Less: QCD relief	Wasted	Wasted	(X)
Taxable total profits (TTP)	0	0	X

Exam focus

Notes:

(i) No marks awarded if capital losses are deducted anywhere other than from chargeable gains.

(ii) The CY trading loss is set off in the order 1, 2, 3, however claims are optional.

(iii) Offset must be against total profits before QCD relief but can be restricted to utilise QCDs.

Approach to a loss relief question

Prepare a TTP pro forma (as above) for the relevant accounting periods

Enter the various amounts of income and gains into the pro forma, remembering to deduct any capital losses (current year or brought forward) from any chargeable gains

Where there is more than one trading loss, deal with the earliest loss first

Consider whether to claim relief against total profits. Remember that you cannot carry back the loss unless you make a current year claim first

After making any claim against total profits, carry forward any remaining loss against future total profits

Complete a loss memorandum working showing how the loss has been relieved and specify any amounts to be carried forward

Exam focus

If a question asks for relief for a trading loss 'as soon as possible' this means you must use the loss against current year total profits and then carry it back 12 months.

Terminal loss relief

Definition

Terminal loss
= loss in final 12 months of trading

- Relieve in current AP first, then
- Carry back against total profits (before QCD relief) of three years preceding loss making period (LIFO basis).

Exam focus

One of the 15 mark questions in part B will always be on corporation tax. It will usually contain a standard corporation tax computation.

However, it may also include trading income adjustments, capital allowances, administration and loss relief claims.

chapter

11

VAT – scope, basics and registration

In this chapter

- VAT – how it works.
- Sources of information.
- Communicating with HMRC.
- Registration.
- Deregistration.
- Exempt and zero-rated supplies.
- Rate of VAT.
- Accounting for VAT.

VAT – how it works

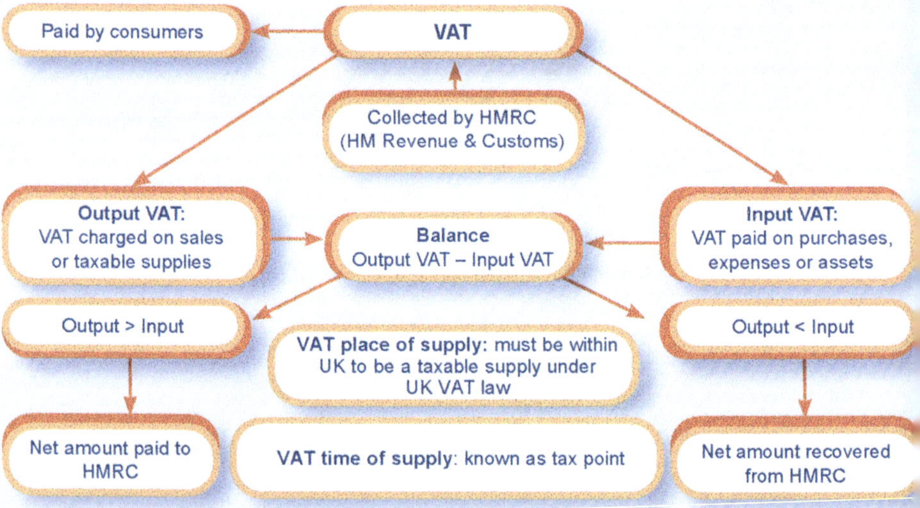

Sources of information

Legislation

- The main source of law on VAT is the VAT Act 1994 as amended by annual Finance Acts and other regulations issued by Parliament.

HMRC website

VAT guide

- HMRC website: VAT Guide Notice 700 is the main guide to VAT rules and procedures.

Communicating with HMRC

VAT helpline

- Telephone helpline.
- Taxpayers can also email or write to HMRC.
- Advisable if contentious issue.
- HMRC expect taxpayers to check information available on website and in VAT guide.

Registration

	Historic test	Future test
Test	Taxable turnover > £90,000 in last 12 months.	Taxable turnover in next 30 days (in isolation) > £90,000.
Notify	Within 30 days of end of month when threshold exceeded.	By end of 30-day period in which threshold will be exceeded.
Registration effective	From 1st day of the second month after taxable supplies exceeded the threshold.	From beginning of 30 day period in which threshold will be exceeded (i.e. backdated to start of 30 day period).
Example	Trader exceeds threshold at 31 Oct 2025. Notify HMRC by 30 Nov 2025. Registration effective from 1 Dec 2025.	On 1 Oct 2025, trader expects to make over £90,000 of taxable supplies in Oct 2025. Notify by 30 Oct 2025. Registration effective from 1 Oct 2025.

Key Point

Taxable turnover = standard-rated (SR), reduced-rate and zero-rated (ZR) supplies.

Voluntary registration

- Consider if making:
  - Zero-rated supplies – to recover input tax, or
  - Standard-rated supplies – if significant input tax in start up period.
- Don't register voluntarily if sales are to general public as will need to increase prices.

Exemption from registration

- Can apply for exemption if make only zero-rated supplies.
- Then unable to claim input tax.
- Avoids administrative burden of complying with VAT regulations.

Penalty for late registration

- Pay over all VAT due from date registration was due.
- May have to pay penalty = % VAT due.
- % depends on taxpayer actions e.g. higher penalty for deliberately concealing information.
- % varies from 0% to 100%.

Deregistration

- Can deregister voluntarily if taxable supplies fall below deregistration threshold of £88,000.
- Must deregister within 30 days of ceasing to make taxable supplies.

Exempt and zero-rated supplies

Zero-rated supplies	Exempt supplies
• Taxable but charged at 0% • Trader can register and reclaim input tax	• Not taxable • Trader can't register and can't reclaim input tax
Examples	**Examples**
Food, unless supplied in course of catering Books and newspapers (including electronic publications) Drugs, medicines Construction of new buildings Public transport Charities Children's clothing and footwear	Land (but not all buildings) Insurance premiums Postal services Betting/gaming/lotteries Financial services (e.g. loans, banking services) Education provided by schools and universities Health and welfare

Rate of VAT

Standard-rate – 20%

Reduced-rate – 5% (awareness only)

Exam focus

When calculating VAT apply

- 20% if given VAT-exclusive amount
- 1/6 if given VAT-inclusive amount

Accounting for VAT

Tax point	Basic = date services are supplied or goods are made available. Use earlier of date of invoice or date of payment if occurs prior to basic tax point; or if not, use invoice date if within 14 days after basic tax point.
Irrecoverable VAT	Cannot recover input VAT on entertaining expenses (except entertaining staff or overseas customers) or motor cars (unless car used wholly for business purposes). Only 50% of input VAT recoverable on leased cars with any private use.
Impaired debts	Recover, provided written off in the accounts and at least six months has elapsed since payment due.
Discounts	Calculate VAT on price net of any discount actually given.
Pre-registration input VAT	Recoverable on services supplied in the six months prior to registration and goods acquired in the four years prior to registration, if still held.
Records	Retain digital copies of all VAT invoices for six years.
Invoices	Need to contain an identifying number, the date of supply, the supplier's name, address and VAT registration number, the customer's name and address, details of the type of supply, the value and rate of VAT for each supply, the total VAT-exclusive amount, and the amount of VAT payable.

Fuel for private use

- All input VAT on cost of fuel = recoverable
- Output VAT:

	Charged on:
– Where full cost reimbursed by the employee / owner	– Cost of fuel reimbursed
– If employee does not reimburse the employer	– Fuel scale charge – depends on CO_2 emissions of car – given in examination

chapter

12

VAT – accounting schemes and returns

In this chapter

- Special accounting schemes.
- Errors on VAT returns.
- Completing the VAT return.
- Effect of a VAT rate change on a business.

Special accounting schemes

Cash accounting

- Account for VAT on basis of cash receipts and payments.
- Eligible to join scheme if taxable turnover does not exceed £1,350,000 p.a.
- All returns and payments must be up to date.
- Automatic relief for impairment losses.
- Must leave scheme once taxable turnover exceeds £1,600,000 p.a.
- No VAT offences in the previous 12 months.

Annual accounting

- One VAT return per year.
- Eligible to join scheme if taxable turnover does not exceed £1,350,000 p.a.
- All returns and payments must be up to date.
- Submit return within two months after the end of the annual VAT period.
- Nine payments on account are made at the end of months 4 to 12 of the annual VAT period.
- Each payment on account is 10% of the net VAT liability for the previous year.
- Balancing payment when return is submitted.
- Saves administration time.
- Helps budgeting.
- Must leave scheme once taxable turnover exceeds £1,600,000 p.a.

Flat rate

- Apply a flat rate of VAT to total VAT-inclusive turnover (inclusive of zero-rated and exempt items as well as output VAT).
- First year of VAT registration = allowed a 1% deduction on the flat rate %.
- Eligible if expected taxable turnover for the next 12 months does not exceed £150,000.
- No recovery of input tax.
- Must leave scheme once taxable turnover (including VAT) for previous 12 months exceeds £230,000.
- Saves administration time.

Errors on VAT returns

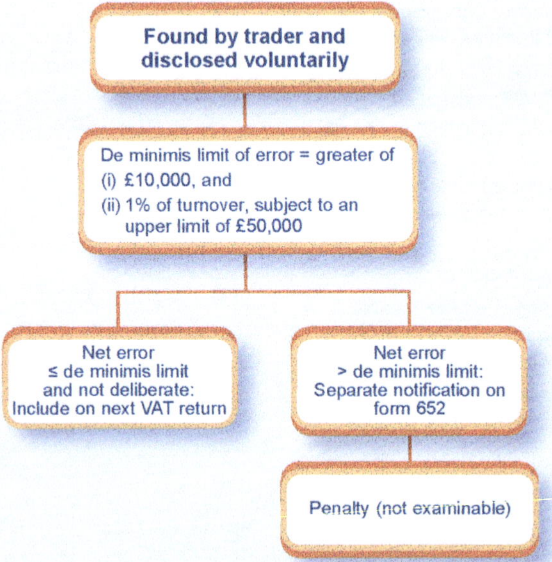

Completing the VAT return

The VAT account

- The main source of information for the VAT return.
- Must be maintained to show the amount due to or from HMRC at the end of each quarter.
- The balance on the VAT account should agree to the balance of VAT payable/ reclaimable on the VAT return.
- Submitted quarterly in electronic form.
- Due by one month and seven days after the end of the quarter.
- Payment due by same date.

Pro forma VAT return

Box 1	VAT due in this period on sales and other outputs.	
Box 4	VAT reclaimed in the period on purchases and other inputs.	
Box 5	Net VAT to be paid to HM Revenue & Customs or reclaimed by you.	
Box 6	Total value of sales and all other outputs excluding any VAT.	
Box 7	Total value of purchases and all other inputs excluding any VAT.	

Notes:

- The relevant box numbers will be provided in the examination in a VAT return question.
- Previous errors which are being corrected on the current return must be included with output VAT in Box 1.
- Impairment loss relief should be included with input VAT in Box 4.
- Zero-rated supplies and purchases should be included with other standard-rated supplies and purchases in Boxes 6 and 7.

VAT computation pro forma

	£	£
Output VAT		
On standard-rated sales		X
On zero-rated sales		0
On fuel scale charge		X
Input VAT		
On inventory purchases	X	
On business expenses (unless irrecoverable)	X	
On plant, and cars with 100% business use	X	
On Impaired debts	X	
	——	(X)
		——
VAT payable or repayable		X/(X)
		——

Effect of a VAT rate change on a business

Generally:

- Sales invoices need to use correct rate of VAT.
- Sales prices used in quotes/pricing invoices must include correct rate of VAT.
- Prices displayed to the public must be correct.
- Staff expense claims must reclaim correct rate of VAT.
- Input VAT reclaimed for purchases and expenses should be the figure shown on the invoice.
- Business may choose to maintain current prices and absorb the VAT increase/ decrease in their profits.

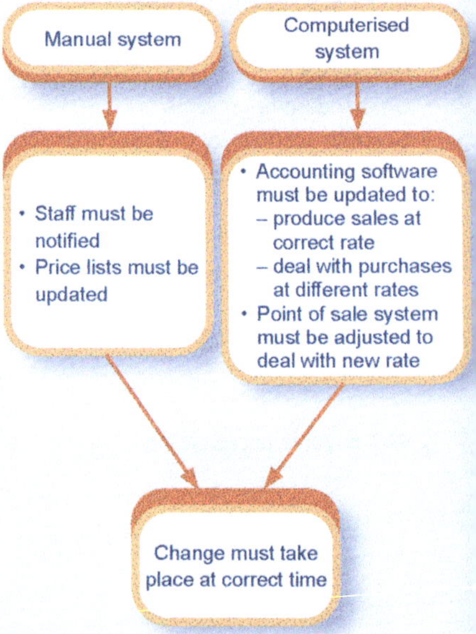

Informing staff

The following staff within a business would need to be told about a rate change and its effects:

IT department staff	To ensure relevant changes are made to computerised accounting system
Sales ledger staff	To raise or check sales invoices correctly
Purchase ledger staff	So they can check purchase invoices correctly
Sales staff	To ensure customers are given correct prices
Marketing department staff	So any new brochures or publicity material is correct
Staff generally	To ensure expense claims are made correctly

chapter

13

Self-assessment

In this chapter

- Self-assessment for companies.
- Appeals.
- Self-assessment for individuals.
- Filing dates.
- Duties and responsibilities.

Self-assessment for companies

Payment dates

Normal date	• Nine months and one day after **end** of AP
'Large' companies (see below)	• Four quarterly instalments • on 14th of months 7, 10, 13 & 16 after **start** of AP • based on estimated liability for the year

Definition of a 'large' company

A 'large' company is one with profits of more than £1,500,000 but no more than £20 million.

- For FTX 'profits' are the same as taxable total profits.
- The £1,500,000 is time apportioned for short accounting periods.
- 'Very large' companies with profits > £20 million are not examinable.

Long periods of account

- Payment dates are based on an accounting period, rather than the period of account.
- A long period of account will have two separate payment dates, one of which may be the normal date and one may be instalments.

Example

If AP ends on 31 December 2025:

- Company which is not large pays all CT on 1 October 2026.
- Large company pays ¼ of estimate on 14 July 2025, 14 October 2025, 14 January 2026 and 14 April 2026.
  Must revise estimate and ensure full liability paid by 14 April 2026.

Interest is charged/paid on under/overpaid tax.
Dealt with as non-trading interest paid or non-trading interest income in TTP.

Exam focus

The precise due date must be given in order to earn a mark in the examination.

Corporation tax return filing date

Required to file a tax return (CT600) when company receives a notice.

↓ If not received

Company must notify HMRC within 12 months of the accounting period otherwise late notification penalty can be charged.

↓ Return must be made

Within 12 months of the end of the period or, if later, three months from the date of the notice requiring the return.

Filing the return

- The return must be filed online.
- The return must be accompanied by accounts.
- The accounts must be filed online using eXtensible Business Reporting Language (iXBRL).
- iXBRL tags information electronically making it easier for computer analysis.

Penalties for late filing

Period of delay	Penalty
Up to 3 months	£100 (or £500 if the previous two returns were late)
3 to 6 months	£200 (or £1,000 if the previous two returns were late)
6 to 12 months	£200 as above, plus 10% of any tax still unpaid six months after the filing date
Over 12 months	£200 as above, plus 20% of any tax still unpaid six months after the filing date

Example

XYZ Ltd's accounting period ends on 31 December 2024.

Provided HMRC issues the return prior to 30 September 2025, it must be filed by 31 December 2025.

If it is not submitted until 31 August 2026, XYZ Ltd will be liable to a penalty of £200 and 10% of any tax outstanding on 30 June 2026.

Amendments

- The company may amend its return within 12 months of the due filing date.
- HMRC may correct obvious errors and anything else which it believes to be incorrect by reference to the information that it holds, within nine months of the date the return was filed.

e.g

Example

Continuing with the above example of XYZ Ltd, the company has until 31 December 2026 to make any amendments.

However, HMRC can correct obvious errors up to 31 May 2027.

Records

Must be kept for at least six years after the end of the accounting period.

Penalties for late notification and incorrect returns

Behaviour	Penalty as % of revenue lost
Mistake	No penalty
Failure to take reasonable care	30%
Deliberate understatement	70%
Deliberate understatement with concealment	100%

- Penalties can be reduced where taxpayer makes full disclosure and cooperates with HMRC to establish the amount of tax unpaid.
- These penalties also apply for income tax and VAT.
- These penalties are provided in the tax tables available in the examination.

Appeals

- Taxpayer's appeals to resolve disputes with HMRC are to the Tax Chamber of the Tribunal.
- First tier used for the majority of cases.
- Upper tier used for more complex cases and for appeals from the first tier.
- Appeals on points of law (not fact) are allowed to the Court of Appeal and Supreme Court.
- Taxpayers can also request a review of their case by a different HMRC officer as an alternative to an appeal.
- The appeal procedure is the same for individuals.

Self-assessment for individuals

Payments on account (POAs)

- POAs are based on the IT and class 4 NIC liability of the previous year (i.e. 2025/26 POAs are based on 2024/25 figures).
- The previous year's liability, net of PAYE, is known as the relevant amount.
- Each POA is 50% of the relevant amount.
- The due dates for POAs for 2025/26 are:
  1st POA – 31 January 2026
  2nd POA – 31 July 2026
- No POAs are required for CGT.
- POAs are not required if:
  - the relevant amount is < £1,000, or
  - more than 80% of the liability for the previous year was deducted through PAYE.

Balancing payment

- The balancing payment is due on 31 January following the tax year.

  For 2025/26 this will be 31 January 2027.
- The balancing payment is:

  Total tax liability for the year (income tax, class 4 NICs and CGT) less PAYE and POAs.
- A balancing repayment may be due instead.

Penalties for late payment

Interest	• Based on the difference between the amount which should have been paid and the amount actually paid. • Calculated on a daily basis, (however calculations will not be required in the examination).
Penalty	• If tax is not paid until more than 30 days after due date – 5% of tax unpaid. • If tax is still unpaid six months after due date – further 5% of tax unpaid. • If tax is still unpaid twelve months after due date – further 5% of tax unpaid. • This penalty does not apply to late payments on account.

Filing dates

The filing date depends on whether the taxpayer is submitting a paper return or an online return.

Paper returns

- The return for 2025/26 must be submitted by 31 October 2026 or, if later, three months after the issue of a notice to file a return.
- HMRC will calculate the tax liability in this case.

Online returns

- Taxpayers who submit their return online have until 31 January following the end of tax year to do so, i.e. by 31 January 2027 for 2025/26 (or, if later, three months after the issue of the notice to file a return).
- A self-assessment of the tax liability is calculated automatically if the return is filed online.

Incorrect returns

- A penalty can be charged (as for corporation tax).

Exam focus

It is important in the examination to state the precise date, including the year, for return submission dates.

Penalties for late filing

Penalty	• £100 if the return is outstanding after 31 January following the tax year. • If the return is more than three months late then a daily penalty of £10 per day can be charged for a maximum of 90 days. • If the return is still outstanding six months after the due date (i.e. after 31 July), then a penalty of 5% of the tax due will also be charged (minimum penalty £300). • When the return is more than 12 months late, a further penalty of 5% of the tax due can be charged (minimum penalty £300). If HMRC consider the failure to be deliberate, then a higher penalty can be charged.

Other matters

Notification	• The time limit for notifying HMRC of chargeability is six months from the end of the tax year in which the liability arises. Failure to notify attracts a penalty as for corporation tax.
Amendments	• The taxpayer can amend the return within 12 months of the 31 January filing date.
Records	• Business records must be retained for five years after the 31 January filing date (i.e. 31 January 2032 for 2025/26). • Non-business taxpayers should normally retain records for 12 months after the 31 January filing date (i.e. 31 January 2028 for 2025/26). • A penalty of up to £3,000 may be charged for failure to keep or retain adequate records.

Duties and responsibilities

- An ACCA tax adviser has duties and responsibilities to:
  - The client.
  - HM Revenue & Customs.
  - ACCA.
- ACCA's Guidelines on Professional Ethics sets out fundamental principles:

Objectivity
Professional behaviour
Professional competence and due care
Integrity
Confidentiality

Key Point

Remember: OPPIC

Confidentiality

- A tax adviser has an overriding duty of confidentiality towards a client.
- No information should be disclosed to a third party without the client's consent.
- Whilst acting in the client's best interest, the tax adviser must deal with HMRC in an open and constructive manner.
- Duty of confidentiality only overridden where there is a legal, regulatory or professional duty to disclose (e.g. where money laundering is suspected).

Tax advice

- In providing tax advice and preparing tax returns a tax adviser must:
  - Act in the best interest of the client.
  - Ensure services comply with the law and are carried out competently.
- Advice must not be given or associated with any communication that is believed to be false or misleading.

Errors and non-disclosure

If tax adviser finds material error or that client has not disclosed all income then:

(1) Must notify client of consequences of not correcting error or not disclosing all income (e.g. interest, penalties and in some cases prosecution) and advise disclosure.

(2) If client will not disclose then adviser must cease to act for client.

(3) Write to HMRC stating that they have ceased to act for the client but without explaining the reason.

(4) Consider whether a report should be made under Money Laundering regulations.

Index

A

B

C

D

E

F